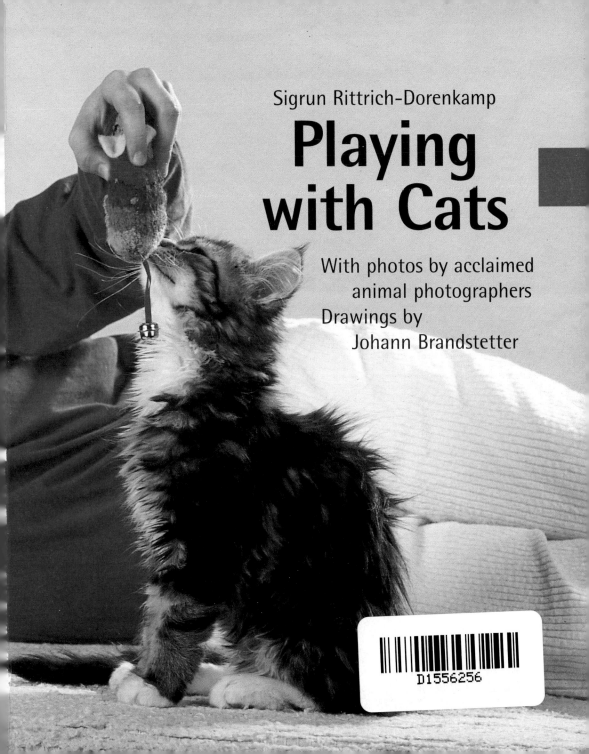

Sigrun Rittrich-Dorenkamp

Playing
with Cats

With photos by acclaimed
animal photographers
Drawings by
Johann Brandstetter

CONTENTS

What Cats Are Like 4

Rules of Play 6

Understanding Cat Behavior 9

Cats Tame People 9

Special Abilities of Cats 9

How Cats Learn 11

Training Kittens 12

What Adult Cats Can Learn 13

Cat Language 14

Chart: Understanding Cat Language 15

How Cats Play 18

Chart: A Kitten's Stages of Development 19

Behavior Interpreter 20

The Right Way to Play with Cats 25

Why Is It Important to Play? 25

Keeping Indoor Cats Occupied 25

TIP: Play Is Soothing to the Soul 26

Training with Games 27

Checklist: Is My Cat Fit? 28

Playing with Indoor Cats that Are Kept Alone 28

Playing with Several Cats 29

Playing with Cats that Run Free 31

Playing with Kittens 31

Playing with Older Cats 31

TIP: Developing Agility and Intelligence 31

Keeping Track of Your Cat's Health 33

The Right Rewards 33

A Practical Living Space for Your Cat 34

Differences Among Breeds 36

Test: How Does My Cat Like to Play? 38

Many Cats Don't Like to Play 40

Playing with Problem Cats 41

Helping Your Cat to Adjust 42

Fun Cat Games 45

Appropriate Toys 45

Commercially Made Toys 45

TIP: Getting the Cat
Used to a Leash 46

There Are Cat Toys in
Every House 47

Keeping Play Safe 49

Practical Advice:
Children and Cats 50

What Kinds of Games
Are There? 52

Teaching Little Tricks 56

HOW-TO: Physical Fitness 58

Index 60

Appendix 62

EXPERT ADVICE 64

WHAT CATS ARE LIKE

- **Predators with a strong hunting instinct**
- **Nimble climbers and talented hunters**
- **Curious and yet cautious**
- **Loners and yet sociable**
- **Refuse to be forced to do anything against their will, and don't like to be restricted**
- **Strong willed and self-confident**
- **Very adaptable—but only when they choose to be**
- **Active during the day and night**
- **Love to cuddle and play for extended periods**

Cats are among the most beloved house pets, and there are millions and millions of them throughout North America, Europe, and other parts of the world. In practically one out of every three households there is one of these fascinating, mysterious creatures that seem to unite so many contradictions in a single being. Even though they are cuddly and affectionate, these small predators can unsheathe their claws in the twinkling of an eye. With their strong will and independence, they refuse to let humans dominate them. House cats have not forgotten the natural behavior of their wild relatives. At the same time, they are conceivably the nicest, most interesting, cleanest, and most intelligent animal friends and housemates. Thanks to their great adaptability, cats can be kept entirely indoors if need be, despite their reputation for independence, assuming that the owners devote some time to them and play with them every day.

RULES OF PLAY

1 In playing, cats like to live out their natural instincts: eyeing and watching the prey, creeping up on it, and catching it.

2 Pet stores offer a broad selection of appropriate toys. You should avoid choosing small balls or pieces that might get swallowed.

3 Let your cat play with a ball of yarn only under close supervision. It could get tangled up in the yarn or even strangle itself.

4 Sometimes play quickly turns serious. When the victim is your hand, don't pull back in fright, or you'll get some nasty scratches. Keep still until the cat calms down. It will quickly realize that it has gone too far.

5 Before you get too rowdy with your cat, you should remove objects that could tip over easily, and protect chair arms with a blanket. The same applies when several kittens are playing at hunting in the house.

6 Even though cats are really nocturnal, they generally adapt without difficulty to the family's daytime routine. If you play at regular times during the day, it's easier for them to regulate their inner clock.

7 If your cat sometimes doesn't feel like playing, don't force it. Maybe it needs a rest. But if the cat continues ot be reluctant, it may be sick, and you should take it to a veterinarian.

Life Is a Game

At least that's what it looks like from a cat's viewpoint. Kittens learn all about hunting by playing. Playing at hunting is also vitally important for adult cats if they can't live out their hunting instinct outdoors. Play takes the place of catching real prey. Without a chance to satisfy this natural drive, serious behavior problems can crop up. Housebound cats need plenty of attention and active play several times a day from their humans. A ball, a bundle of feathers, or a toy mouse can serve as acceptable prey. Even a human hand or a toe under the bed covers is the perfect quarry in a cat's view. If you want to avoid real injuries, you should be sure that your hand is never used as a plaything; rather, it should be used only to stroke, fondle, and feed. Especially with cats that are allowed to run free, and that can come and go as they please, games and activities are tremendously useful in fostering a harmonious relationship between human and animal.

UNDERSTANDING CAT BEHAVIOR

By nature, cats love to play, and their motivation to play is inseparable from their hunting instinct. When they live under the same roof with humans, it's our duty to give them a chance to exercise this instinct. To enjoy a harmonious relationship with your cat, you have to begin by understanding its behavior.

Cats Tame People

Cats are happy to seek out "their people," the ones they want to live with. That's often still the case in rural areas. As early as eight to nine thousand years ago wild cats voluntarily connected with humans. In their granaries there were plenty of mice and rats, and cats recognized these places as ideal hunting grounds. In addition, human housing offered shelter and warmth. Although the cats pursued their own agenda, they were also useful to the humans. So it wasn't people who domesticated cats. These intelligent hunters effectively domesticated themselves by seeking out people to be their partners.

In the many millennia since cats "made up their minds" to help people contain the plague of mice and rats, they have scarcely changed. Today, just as then, they go their own way. They came to people voluntarily, and even now humans have to earn the affection of their cats. If they fall into the bad graces of their cats, the creatures clearly show their displeasure or simply leave them. They never follow in blind obedience. This is surely the reason why many people have a rather ambivalent relationship with cats. They simply can't come to grips with the obvious independence of the velvety-pawed creatures. Good cat people are tolerant, don't try to force cats into doing things that they won't do willingly, and give them as much freedom as possible. These people aren't awkward or abrupt in their movements, and their voices are not loud.

Cats Are Still Hunters

Today, just as in the past, cats that live in the wild primarily eat small rodents. The hunting instinct is so highly developed that even when its belly is full, a cat is always ready to stalk new prey—even if it doesn't like mice. No one can break cats of hunting. If today's cats have no opportunity to go after real game—except perhaps for an occasional fly—they look for substitutes when they play.

Special Abilities of Cats

Their supple, powerful bodies, their great jumping ability, their long, strong canine teeth, and their movable claws make cats one of the most highly developed predators.

Elegance and Strength

Cats have about 240 light but strong bones and more than 500 muscles to thank for their agility and speed. Their spine is especially supple. Cats can turn their head up to 180 degrees, and they are so flexible that when they clean themselves, they can effortlessly reach almost every part of their body. They can jump in any direction, even backward, from a standing position. Without a running start, they can jump up five times their length. Although they can easily get over obstacles six feet (two meters) high, they hate to jump down or to climb down headfirst.

In a free fall, cats can always twist around so that they land on all fours, at least as long as they have enough time to make the turn. But despite that, they can sustain injuries if they fall too far. Cats are outstanding sprinters and jumpers, but they're not endurance athletes.

They can't keep up their high performance for very long. As a result, they never pursue their prey very long if it manages to escape. And if they have to make a getaway, they almost always choose an upward escape route.

Soft Paws and Sharp Claws

The claws are a cat's most potent weapon. They are protected from wear and kept sharp as needles because muscles and tendons retract them into skin sheaths in the pads. They are extended as fast as lightning when a cat pounces on prey, fights, or climbs. The pads (five on the front feet and four on the rear) have soft cushions, and in combination with the movable toes, they enable cats to walk very smoothly. Cats take care of their own claws. They use their teeth to remove old layers and keep the claws in good condition. Scratching on a tree keeps them good and sharp and keeps them from getting too long. To keep your tame tiger from wanting to scratch your furniture and carpets, it's important to provide it with an

Cats jump on their prey with great accuracy.

alternative such as a scratching post (see pages 35 and 43). This can be used for more than sharpening claws; it can be turned into a favorite playground by adding balls, ropes, perches, and cubbyholes.

Dangerous Teeth and a Raspy Tongue

Even though cats have only thirty teeth—fewer than other four-legged meat eaters—their bite is a very dangerous weapon. They use their canine teeth to catch their quarry and kill it. With their scissorlike molars they cut up the prey before they gulp the pieces down. The tiny incisors, six each on top and bottom, are used for nibbling and for taking care of coat and claws.

The rough tongue, which is covered with papillae, helps scrape meat from bones and serves as a brush in taking care of the coat.

A Cat's Vision

A cat's big, shiny eyes are particularly appealing to us. The pupils contract to narrow slits in bright light, and expand to huge discs in the darkness. Cats can discern shapes, outlines, and movements in low light and at night. A portion of the available light is reflected by a mirrorlike layer in the back of the eye; it acts like a reflector and makes a cat's eyes shine at night. Cats can see about ten yards/meters. Since they also have a full 180-degree field of view, there's not much that escapes their attention.

A Cat's Sense of Hearing

A cat's sense of hearing far exceeds our conception. Cat ears can pick up vibrations of 20 Hertz (a very low pitch) up to 65,000 Hertz (a very high pitch in the realm of ultrasound). We humans hear only up to about 20,000 Hertz as children, and a good deal less as adults. Cats can not only hear tones, but also clearly determine where they come from and how far away they are. That enables them to find and catch a mouse even when they can't see it.

Sensitive Whiskers

Whiskers on the muzzle and cheeks and other sensor hairs on the eyebrows and the back of the forelegs provide information to sensitive nerves about vibrations, temperature, and air pressure. They enable cats to find their way even in complete darkness. Cats fan their whiskers outward and forward to test such things as the temperature and the nature of an unknown object.

A Good Nose

The sense of smell likewise plays an important part in a cat's life. Newborn kittens use it to find the mother's nipples, and later it provides information about territorial boundaries, other cats, sexual activity, edibles, and much more. Some scents provide cats with sensual pleasure, such as catnip and valerian. When such fragrant ingredients are contained in cat toys, many cats go wild for them (see page 45).

How Cats Learn

Cats continue to learn from before birth right up to the time they die. They have a great capacity for learning. They try out new experiences and adapt their behavior specifically. They can learn by imitation; that is, they imitate what the mother, another cat, or a human demonstrates for them. But if there is no model, they can still grope their way along by trial and error. In so doing, cats will try various alternatives. If one of them works, the cat will use it in similar circumstances in the future. Cats don't forget what they have once learned. They are very open to new experiences, but they cling to behaviors that they have found to be useful. They are willing to unlearn something only when a totally new situation arises, such as unfamiliar surroundings. Then they learn very quickly and adjust to the new situation.

Providing Positive Stimuli

Cats can reasonably be considered to be clever and intelligent animals. But that doesn't mean that they have any interest in obeying commands from people. They simply can't see why they ought to obey. Forbidding, scolding,

and punishing are totally pointless. On the other hand, sometimes cats are ready to respond to human stimuli—of their own free will, of course. If the person is in a position to make these stimuli palatable, it's a done deal. The cat needs to be able to link something positive to the desired behavior—such as a treat, some petting, or playing—and then it will comply willingly. It's even possible to motivate a cat to do some little tricks (see pages 56–57). Conversely, linking an unpleasant experience, such as a stream of water from a squirt bottle, to undesirable behavior can also work wonders. But the cat should not recognize that type of negative experience as a punishment that comes from a person.

Training Kittens

In the second and third month of life, kittens learn everything they need to know by playing: creeping stealthily, estimating distances, jumping, catching, pursuing, the death bite, eating prey, climbing and balancing, fighting, and fleeing. They experience the difference between friends and enemies, and what's edible and what's not. They imitate their mother—how she grooms herself, sharpens her claws, and buries her urine and droppings. They don't

A round basket with a little ball suspended in it is a perfect plaything.

sleep very much at this point. At the age of eleven to twelve weeks a young kitten already possesses all the basic techniques of a full-grown cat. But even if the kitten has never learned how to hunt mice, perhaps because it has grown up exclusively indoors, it can later teach itself how to hunt living prey. Just the same, not all these cats master the death bite, and many of them don't regard the caught mouse as food.

What Adult Cats Can Learn

Even older cats are still capable of learning, and they still like to play. Their reactions are just as good as those of younger cats. Only their movements are no longer as explosive. Even older cats need activity and exercise to stay healthy and feel good. In the wild, cats

Following the mother on an expedition through the yard—that's exciting!

must continue to hunt mice even in old age in order to survive.

Well-cared-for cats can live to the age of about fifteen to twenty. But starting as early as age ten the aging process becomes evident: The cat becomes more subdued, sleeps a lot, avoids conflicts, and is less receptive to new things. How ready it is to learn something new or to try a new game depends largely on whether it has lazed around on the sofa for the whole year, or has experienced new stimuli and has therefore remained physically and mentally fit.

Cat Language

For daily dialogue and play with your cat, it will be helpful for you to know as much as possible of its language. Few animals have as rich a repertory of complex communicative strategies as cats do. They have at least four means of communication: sound, facial expressions, body language, and scent signals. They are very adept at using them individually or in combinations.

Voice

Meowing is surely the most familiar cat sound. A short, clear meow sounds whenever the cat wants something, and whenever it feels disturbed or unhappy with some situation. Meowing for a partner is very different from that. When a mother calls for her young, the sound is likewise different. If she brings them prey, she even distinguishes vocally among different types of treats: Mice are announced differently than a dangerous rat. In addition, every cat has its own unmistakable voice.

In addition to meowing, cats have a rich variety of other sounds: They can yell and shriek or give an ear-splitting howl, such as in great distress, in a fight, or in mating. They can wail hoarsely if they are sick. They can wail or snarl if a fly or a bird is beyond reach. They greet by cooing amicably in several registers. They also gather their young by uttering a high-pitched coo. Mixed with mewing, those sounds become a sort of "talk." Some cats are regular chatterboxes, and others are more tight-lipped.

In addition to endless variations on these vocal tones, cats have plenty of unvoiced sounds at their disposal: They purr when they feel good, and also to soothe and calm themselves down. They hiss as a warning and to defend themselves. If a cat wants to attack or show its strength, it will snarl or even rumble angrily.

Facial Expressions

Cats emphasize many utterances with corresponding facial expressions. For example, when they hiss, they open their mouth halfway, pull back the upper lip, pull the ears back, and lay them flat or raise them up, depending on the situation.

Cats greet their people by rubbing with their head.

Understanding Cat Language

Body Language	Facial Expression	Voice	Meaning
Lying down, relaxed, kneading with front paws	Eyes and ears still, ears turned slightly outward	Purring	I'm happy to be with you; keep doing what you're doing.
Rubbing against your legs, rubbing head against your leg, tail held high	As above, eyes half closed	Purring or meowing invitingly	Play and cuddle with me! Or, give me something to eat.
Head raised, body and legs straight, tail high	Eyes and ears still, ears turned slightly outward	Meowing and cooing	Friendly greeting: What shall we do now?
Body tense, legs straight, tip of tail twitching	Ears pointed forward, eyes open wide, whiskers fanned out toward the front	Short, clear meowing, snarling, or moaning	Attentiveness: What's going on? How do I get there? Will you help me?
Back slightly arched, tail lifted but curved downward, hackles raised, forefoot raised	Ears pointed slightly outward, whiskers fanned out to the front, head to one side, eyes directed forward	Mewing and slight snarling	Playful attack threat: Who is the stronger? Let's scrap!
Back straight, hackles raised, legs pulled back, tail high and whipping back and forth	Ears held high but pulled back, head raised, pupils contracted	Deep snarling, rumbling, even changing to a sirenlike wail	Watch out, I'm about to attack; better get away while you can!
Back arched, rear legs tucked under, tail flailing, hackles raised	Ears laid flat to the side, head low, whiskers tightly pulled back, dilated pupils	Hissing, spitting, shrieking, squealing	I'm going to defend myself; leave me alone! (But if I can I'll make a quick getaway.)

The kitten uses its paw to test the waters.

They also narrow their pupils when they want to threaten to attack. Dilated pupils denote anxiety and defensiveness.

When a cat aggressively approaches an antagonist, the ears are held high and turned to the rear, and the head is turned to one side. Even the position of the whiskers reveals that cat's mood: If they're pulled back, they communicate anxiety; fanned far to the front, they denote intense alertness.

Body Language

Cats broadcast unmistakable signals with the position of their tail, varied postures of head and body, and the raising of their fur.

If you want to know what kind of mood your domestic tiger is in, pay particular attention to the tail: When the cat approaches you in a good mood, the tail is still and held high. Quick back-and-forth movements signal excitement. An attack is immediately preceded by a quick raising of the tail and flailing it back and forth. With threatening behavior, the tail is slightly lowered and points straight down; only the tip moves back and forth. The fur on the tail and the back is raised. If the cat feels fairly self-confident, its torso stays relatively straight.

The cat waits for the right instant to jump into a tree.

But if it's frightened or ready to defend itself, it arches its back and raises all its hackles to make itself bigger.

Things can get dangerous when the tail is held stiff and high and shaped like a bottle brush. If the hind legs are tucked in, it's a sign of anxiety, uncertainty, and even tense readiness to attack. Holding the legs straight is a sign of self-confidence and superiority. Cats also display their strength in front of other cats by sharpening their claws or spraying urine.

Scent Signals

We are only too familiar with the propensity of male cats to spray urine onto walls, posts, and bushes. People can hardly stand this smell. But cats also have many discreet ways of communicating through scent. They have glands in the skin of their cheeks, chin, foot pads, and back that secrete scents that we can't even detect. When they touch each other, they transfer scents to one another. Rubbing their head, cheeks, and bodies are typical behaviors that accomplish this. Scent messages are left even when cats sharpen their claws, and are deposited on objects to communicate the news to other cats.

How Cats Play

Kittens play all day long—they tussle with their siblings, hop up onto the mother, and hunt imaginary prey. That helps them learn everything that they will later need in life. For them playing and learning are inseparably linked to each other.

But even adult cats like to play a lot. House cats live out their hunting instinct by playing when they pounce on, hunt, catch, fling away, and carry off a ball, a bundle of feathers, a ball of paper, or a piece of string. Cats that run free also like to play—but their prey is real.

Learning from the Mother Cat by Playing

In the first two to three months, kittens play with their mother and learn everything they will later need to master life.

As early as the first day of life newborn kittens begin gathering impressions of their surroundings and tailoring their behavior to them. The senses of touch and smell are already well developed, and kittens can identify warmth and the scent of their mother and siblings.

At barely one week old, the little ones react to unknown sounds, especially scratching noises. In three weeks more, those noises cause the kittens to hop in that direction to seize an imaginary prey animal.

At the age of about two weeks, they begin to play, at first rather clumsily, and starting with the fourth week, they leave their basket to go on little expeditions.

Starting at the age of five weeks, kittens can already jump and climb a little. They now dash everywhere and tumble down stairs and over one another.

At this stage the mother cat intensively prepares her offspring for life. She wags the tip of her tail back and forth so the little ones will seize the prey. She rolls with them on the floor, grabs them with her paw, and bites them gently until they squeal. That's how she teaches them to defend themselves.

She brings prey, throws it into the air, catches it again, and inspires the little ones to do the same. At first the mouse she brings is already dead, but soon the mother brings mice that she has only disabled. The kittens are supposed to play with them to train their hunting reflexes. Soon the prey is still able-bodied so that the young ones can catch it for themselves and kill it. If there are no real rodents, the mother may choose substitutes such as a piece of meat, a bug, or a butterfly. The kittens can do more and more every day.

The mother cats watches over her offspring to make sure nothing happens to them as they tussle with one another.

A Kitten's Stages of Development

Age	What the Kitten Can Do
First day of life	Purr while sucking milk
First week of life	Totter on wobbly legs, yell, and struggle to get to the best teat
Second week of life (usually 7 to 14 days)	Eyes open, but still doesn't see much. Recognizes where noises come from.
Third week of life	The kitten becomes lively. It sees more. First clumsy games with siblings.
Fourth and fifth weeks of life	The curious kitten climbs out of its box. The mother brings the first solid food and prey.
Sixth week of life	The kitten now sees clearly, runs, jumps, and climbs.
Seventh to twelfth week of life	The kitten becomes independent. By playing it learns everything it will need to know as an adult.

Playing with Siblings

Starting with their first days, the little kittens tussle with one another to get the best teat. As soon as their eyes open, they begin to paw their siblings—at first very tentatively, and then with more resolve. Soon they scrap, stalk, creep after, fend off, and hurl themselves onto their brothers and sisters like crazy. They arch their backs and jump onto their opponents with tail and hackles raised. They engage in some wild pursuits that culminate in a "battle."

Then the game ends suddenly, the roles change, and the hunted becomes the hunter. Siblings have to serve as rivals, partners, and prey. That's how kittens play and develop all the skills they will need for hunting and self-defense.

BEHAVIOR
INTERPRETER

For play and other activities with your cat, you'll need to understand its behavior.

 My cat does this.

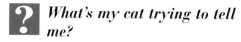 *What's my cat trying to tell me?*

The right response to this behavior

The cat arches its back and raises its fur a little.

It's been alarmed and is ready to defend itself, but at the same time it's curious.

It's better not to touch it now. Speak to it soothingly.

The cat is sound asleep.

It has played enough and is resting.

Best to let it rest.

The cat yawns.

It's not necessarily sleepy, but wants to settle down: "I feel peaceful; please be nice to me."

You may stroke it gently.

The cat creeps along and remains in a tense crouching position.

It has spotted some prey.

Don't disturb it. Even for house cats it's important to be able to live out their hunting instinct.

The cat pulls its ears back and  to the side, and dilates its pupils.

It's ready to defend itself. **?**

Better not touch it, or it may **!** attack. Speak to it gently to calm it down.

The cat has caught a mouse.

? It's carrying out its innate hunting instinct.

! Don't scold the cat. It's proud of its prey.

21

The cat sharpens its claws on a wooden slat.

At the same time it wants to make an impression and leave a scent signal.

Give your cat a place to scratch inside the house, too.

The cat playfully bites your  hand.

It's playing with **?** your hand as if it were another cat.

Don't pull **!** your hand away, or you'll end up with some scratches. It's better to use a toy than your hand.

The kitten is damaging a houseplant.

? It's bored. It doesn't have anything to do.

! Provide appropriate cat toys and pay lots of attention to the kitten.

TIP

Always in the Middle of Things

No matter what you do, your cat always wants to be part of it. When you're trying to read the newspaper, it jumps onto the pages and covers them up. When you try to write something down, it purrs loudly as it climbs onto the paper and tries to catch your pencil. When you sit at the computer, the cat walks on the keyboard and changes all the settings. The cat "helps" the children when they do their homework and helps you prepare the vegetables. When you play the piano, it accompanies you with a run across the keys, and in the morning it's happy to wake you up early so you can play or cuddle with it. Don't scold it. Such playful and affectionate cats need your attention. Include them as much as possible in your daily life. Where feline curiosity really becomes a nuisance (at the dinner table, for example), set clear boundaries and be consistent.

Playing with Other Cats

If you don't have enough time to devote to cuddling and playing with your feline friend every day, you should consider getting a second cat. If you know from the start that you are going to have two cats, it's best to get siblings or at least two young kittens.

Siblings that have grown up together generally get along fine with one another later on and continue to play together.

If a kitten remains with its mother they will likewise continue to live together harmoniously.

Young kittens make friends quite quickly with another unknown cat. If the other cat is also young, it often takes only a few minutes for the two of them to start fighting playfully and chasing each other, or playing with the same toy.

If a young cat meets an older one, there are generally few problems. The young cat will break down all barriers with its high spirits and get the older one to play with it. Most older animals don't act aggressively with unknown younger ones.

Two adult cats find it a little harder to get used to each other. Cats are strong individualists. Many are quite tolerant and make friends with each other after a short while. Then they choose their resting places near each other, tussle and play with each other, and carry out joint expeditions in their territory. Others go their own way and merely put up with the "rival." They are careful not to come too close, and they will never play together.

Still others attack every "intruder" with a fury. The old cat feels insulted, and the new one is totally intimidated. A pile left on the sofa or a puddle on the bed is a sign of protest. In such cases, unfortunately, there is not much chance that the two will ever adjust to each other.

Playing with Other Animals

Cats can also make friends with other animals, but not all house pets are appropriate playmates. Cats generally regard anything that's smaller than they are as prey animals. Larger animals at first frighten them and are regarded as enemies.

Small rodents and birds: There are instances where guinea pigs, hamsters, parakeets, or even mice have lived peaceably with cats. But those are clearly exceptions. Even if the animals have grown up together, there is a great risk that the cat's hunting instinct will suddenly manifest itself, and that the supposed friend will be killed or severely injured.

Rabbits: In the cat's eyes, rabbits are prey animals, even if they are about the same size. Putting a grown cat and a young, little bunny together will almost surely lead to the death of the bunny! A young kitten and a bunny can, however, get quite used to each other. The bunny usually is not afraid of the kitten, and after a short while the two get along fine, even if they speak an entirely different language. They will probably also accept each other even later on. Most usually don't learn how to play many games together, but it's great fun for both of them to chase each other around.

Dogs: Great friendships can grow between cats and dogs, and dogs really are good playmates for cats. Of course that requires a dog that hasn't been trained to chase cats, and the cat that hasn't had bad experiences with dogs. Kittens and puppies most easily get accustomed to one another. But even many grown dogs accept cats as new housemates. Some dogs chase after cats as if they are wild creatures outdoors, but in the house they are the best playmates. And there are dogs that are really crazy about cats. Still others punish them by ignoring them.

Soon the cat and dog have learned each other's language so that there are no further misunderstandings. Then the cat no longer takes the dog's tail wagging as a threat of attack; it's more likely to regard the tail as the perfect toy. And the dog learns to distinguish the cat's growling from its own. Most cats tolerate it when the dog barks too loudly or bears its teeth while playing. And it doesn't bother the dog when it feels the cat's teeth and claws when they romp (see "Helping Your Cat to Adjust," page 42).

Cats that like each other often lie close together and snuggle.

THE RIGHT WAY TO PLAY WITH CATS

For house cats, playing is an important part of life. Whereas cats that run free can exercise their hunting and playing instincts outdoors, indoor cats look to their humans to provide plenty of attention.

Why Is It Important to Play?

In playing, kittens learn everything they need to know in life. The more play the growing ball of fur gets, the more intelligent and agile it becomes. It's born with an instinct to play, and that remains throughout its entire life. Even cats that hunt outdoors play with their captured prey, toss it up, perhaps let it get away so they can catch it again, and shove it with their paw to make it flee. This is how they work off the excitement that has built up during the process of reconnoitering and stalking, reduce stress, and develop their agility.

This hunting and playing instinct has nothing to do with whether or not the little predator is hungry. It's so strong that even cats that are entirely full can't leave a newly discovered mouse alone. And if there is no real prey to be had, they are just as happy to play with some appropriate substitute.

What the heck is that in there? How can I get it out?

Strengthening the Relationship Between Human and Cat

We always get to know our cats better and develop a close and trusting relationship when we play with them. The more we play with our cats, the more trusting and alert they become. Cats and people come to act as partners. Together we can invent new games. We soon know what they like to do and what they don't care for. But cats also adjust to our preferences. If play sessions are set for the same time each day, the cat will be there waiting eagerly. And we soon realize that if the cat is happy and contented, we're also happier and more at ease.

The love that we bestow on our cats is returned to us in ample measure. Our relationship with the cat becomes a source of happiness in life.

Keeping Indoor Cats Occupied

It may seem inappropriate at first glance, but there are lots of good reasons for keeping the little predators indoors. Hundreds of thousands of free-roaming cats are killed by cars and other hazards every year. Indoor cats generally live to a much riper age than free-roaming cats because they are exposed to far fewer dangers.

TIP

Play Is Soothing to the Soul

Daily play and activity with a cat are also good for the human body and soul. Games of pursuit, hide-and-seek, and walks also promote agility for us two-legged creatures. Watching a cat play enthusiastically is engrossing, and it helps us get rid of daily stress and aggravation. It can cheer us up and console us. It gives us a different feeling for time. The cat clearly shows the affection it has for us. It shows us how important we are as partners, and that it places a high value on our company. It fosters our creativity as we invent new games. And there is hardly anything more relaxing than petting a purring cat that has made itself comfortable on our lap. Doctors and psychologists have long known about the comforting and calming effect that cats have on both children and adults.

Thanks to their outstanding adaptability, cats can adjust very well to living entirely indoors, especially if they have gotten used to it from the time they were little. But even a full-grown cat can adjust if it's placed into a new environment. No one needs to have an uneasy conscience about denying a cat unfettered access to the yard, fields, and blocks of houses. However, the cat has to be compensated for that in some way.

House cats that don't have a chance to let off steam and be active for a couple of hours a day are very understimulated. In particular, this affects indoor cats that are kept alone and whose owner is often away. They feel lonely and are bored. The smarter the cat is, the more ill at ease it is about having nothing to do. That type of animal often develops serious behavior problems such as aggressiveness, since it has no other way of getting rid of its pent-up energy. Or else it becomes increasingly dull, overeats, and turns into nothing but an ornamental piece.

House cats need to play at least three to four times more than free-ranging cats.

A cat that's kept alone indoors forms a very close bond with its beloved human. If there are several people in the family and if someone is almost always home, the cat is less likely to feel lonesome.

It's entirely different in the case of a single working person, though. The cat can hardly wait for the human to spend some time with it. The human partner has to be available to play and cuddle with the cat at least after work and on weekends. It needs several hours of activity every day, some attention, and a house that's set up with the cat's needs in mind, with plenty of opportunities for hiding and climbing (see the practical advice on setting up your house for the cat, pages 34–35).

Note: If you're a single working person who doesn't have much time to devote to your cat, it would be better to get two cats to keep each other entertained when you're not there.

Training with Games

It's true that cats don't obey as well as a well-trained dog. That would be entirely contrary to the nature of these individualists. But they can learn, up to a certain point, the type of behavior that is unacceptable, and they are often willing to do things properly. You can use enjoyable games to make the cat easier to train and behave the way you expect. For example, you can get it used to using a scratching post or teach it not to climb up the curtains (see practical advice on Helping Your Cat to Adjust, pages 42–43). If the cat fulfills your wishes appropriately, it should be rewarded with something pleasant. If it does something bad—such as sharpening its claws on the sofa—that must be linked to an unpleasant experience.

If the play becomes too wild and unbridled, you may get to feel your cat's claws, and that may be unintentional on the cat's part. But you have to make it clear from the beginning that the cat has to keep its claws retracted when it plays with humans. Say "Ow!" clearly and use your finger to snap its paw. Connect play to some object that the cat can use to work off its energy.

It can also happen that your cat's mood suddenly changes while you're playing or cuddling with it, and it wants to scratch or bite you. It's not doing anything wrong, but merely reacting true to its kind. When cats play with one another, they likewise strike out with their paws to reestablish needed distance.

Note: If you watch your cat carefully while playing with it or petting it, you'll be able to see when things are getting "dangerous." Stop the game as soon as you see the claws come out and the pupils narrow.

No cat can resist a finger imitating a prey animal as it moves under a blanket.

Checklist
Is My Cat Fit?

1 The cat is slender, with well-developed muscles. You can feel the ribs, but they don't stick out.

2 It has smooth, thick fur, clean ears, and shiny eyes.

3 It's active for several hours a day and plays boisterously.

4 It can easily jump up onto a table in a single bound.

5 It reacts curiously to everything new.

6 It "converses" in cat talk with its human.

7 As it cleans itself with its tongue it can effortlessly reach every part of its body.

8 It purrs when it's patted.

9 If the cat lies around list-lessly, it's either ill or over-weight. You should bring it to a veterinarian.

What Kind of Play and How Much?

If we watch the cat, it will tell us if we're playing and cuddling with it in the right way. Cats develop very individualized preferences for certain games and hiding places. Their need to play also varies widely; it depends on their environment, age, health, and breed.

Playing with Indoor Cats that Are Kept Alone

Cats that are kept exclusively indoors and without the company of a second cat have a heightened need for play. Their human should spend several hours with them every day playing, cuddling, and simply being there. At least an hour, including breaks, should be set aside every day for active games such as wrestling and tumbling. An indoor cat needs three to four times as much play as a cat that runs free in order to satisfy its hunting instinct and need for exercise. Set up your house or apartment so it offers as much variety as possible (see practical advice on an environment for your cat, pages 34–35). But even the best toy is not much use if your cat doesn't get enough of your personal attention.

You can compensate your indoor tiger for its lack of expeditions by taking it for regular walks on a leash. Many cats enjoy that a lot after a certain period of adjustment, provided that the neighborhood is fairly serene and that you allow it enough time and freedom to move around (see pages 46 and 58). But if after several attempts your cat gets no enjoyment out of this, don't try to force the issue.

Playing with Several Cats

Paper bags are perfect hiding places for cats.

If you have two or more cats in your house, they probably will keep each other quite busy. If other partners in play and society are available, the cats don't suffer so much if their human doesn't have enough time for them. Just the same, they love playing with their human partner. The relationship with a human can even become much closer than with another cat.

In a house with two or more kittens, things become a good deal more turbulent than with a single cat. Full-throttle chases over chairs and tables can have a very detrimental effect on furnishings and decorations.

The cats race, gallop, stalk, jump, hop, and scrap, and it's great fun to watch them. But during this wild phase it's a good idea to protect your upholstered furniture by placing blankets over it and moving everything out of the way that could easily be knocked over.

Several cats also like to play together with a ball. The techniques the house cats develop in trapping the ball are enough to make every soccer or handball player green with envy. Pingpong balls and balls of a similar size made of rubber or foam that are available at pet shops are good choices.

It's also exciting to move a toy mouse or similar toy on the end of a string. Which cat is the quickest and most alert? Usually both try to get the toy at the same time. Practicing little tricks such as balancing or jumping through a hoop (see pages 56–57) can also be fun for many cats.

Cats that like each other cuddle for hours at a time and help one another groom. But even when they get along very well together, all cats should have a special room available as a refuge and a primary home, as it were. As a rule of thumb, you should not keep more cats than the number of rooms in your house or apartment. In addition, provide as many hiding places as possible where the cats can sneak in, such as baskets, empty boxes, and perhaps even an open cupboard. Have a number of places available for resting and sleeping. Cats are particularly fond of the soft plush hiding holes that are sold in pet shops; you can place these in various places in your house, even on shelves or in cupboards.

You can easily install special cat perches on windowsills or radiators. They afford the tame tiger a warm sleeping place and a good view of the outdoors. It's also important that every cat have its own litter box and dishes for food and water. Each cat will mark its territory in the house and respect that of the other cats.

An aquarium functions like a cat television and is fascinating to many indoor tigers.

Playing with Cats that Run Free

Cats that are allowed to run free find enough stimuli on their outdoor stalks to satisfy their need for exercise and their hunting instinct. But they are still happy to play with their human in the house, on the porch, or in the yard. They love the company. Even if playing together isn't absolutely necessary for the cat's physical fitness—in contrast to indoor cats—it's still good for the psyche, and it strengthens the relationship between human and cat. The mouser is always glad to come home and doesn't stray so far afield on its expeditions through the territory.

Playing with Kittens

In the first weeks and months a kitten that's kept singly needs lots of attention and activity. A cat is never more active, curious, and capable of learning than when it's young. Play with it as often as possible (as long as it's not sleeping, but at this stage that's rarely the case). It's also a good idea to practice walking the cat on a leash while it's small, but you have to be very patient. Young cats are especially fond of games that involve lots of activity, in which they can run and jump. In addition, they find lots of appealing places to hide, such as cardboard tubes, paper bags, and large boots and pockets.

Playing with Older Cats

The instinct to play lasts well into old age. Even elderly cats in good health like to play. But the games have to be a little more sedate. Wild and crazy games are no longer their thing. The cats are more levelheaded and more serious; they don't squander their energy for nothing. Choose games that involve teasing and catching, in which the cat can catch the prey quickly and dexterously; otherwise it may

TIP

Developing Agility and Intelligence

It's a lot of fun to practice little tricks with your cat, such as having it balance on a board or a thick rope (see pages 56–57). That develops its agility on the one hand, and on the other, it promotes intelligence. Cats that have been exposed to lots of stimuli, have been picked up a lot, and learned many different games in their youth seem to be more intelligent. Try doing new things with your cat! You'll find some ideas to help with this starting on page 45.

quickly lose interest. Change toys more frequently. Include the cat in your daily routine and talk to it a lot. Many older indoor cats need more motivation to play. To keep them physically fit, you should play with them at least an hour a day in addition to cuddling, which older cats really enjoy.

Observing Periods of Activity and Rest

Cats are perfectly suited to high-performance physical activity, but only for short periods of time. Though they have a great need for activity, they are not long-distance runners. Favorite activities of all cats include snoozing, observing, lying in the sun, and sleeping. It's important for us to give them

enough rest. No cat that's roused from a deep sleep will want to play, and it may react rather ungraciously. But if we disturb it when it's only taking a nap, it probably will leap at the opportunity to play.

A cat's main period of activity is normally in the twilight hours of morning and evening and during the night. But cats adapt easily to the family's timetable and gladly play during the day and rest at night.

The daily activities of a free-ranging cat can be tallied in approximately this way: It spends about ten hours sleeping, five to six hours resting, snoozing, cuddling, and lying in the sun, three to four hours grooming, three to five hours prowling around, hunting, and playing,

Little kittens are almost always eager to play—even when they are really tired.

one to two hours dawdling, walking around, and visiting acquaintances, and about half an hour eating and drinking.

An indoor cat, depending on its age and personality, frequently stretches its rest periods out even longer. Additionally, there are of course significant differences among breeds.

Keeping Track of Your Cat's Health

In order to play actively, your cat has to be in good health. If it's not motivated to play for a fairly long time and prefers to hang around listlessly in a corner, then there's something wrong with it. Older cats in particular suffer from many serious complaints, such as liver or kidney disease, which remain undetected for a long time, or painful joints that take away the pleasure of physical exercise. Even a cat that has worms or fleas usually doesn't want to play, because it doesn't feel good. But even younger cats can become ill. Listlessness at play is one of the first signs that the cat is experiencing pain or a fever.

Note: If your cat's behavior changes noticeably and it's no longer inclined to play, take it to a veterinarian as soon as possible. If it's determined that your cat is suffering from some illness, find out from the doctor how much activity it can take. Oftentimes moderate training is good for it and will help it get well.

The Right Rewards

By using snacks as rewards you can facilitate many training processes and make it easier to teach the cat some tricks. But you should avoid getting into the habit of continually giving your cat treats. On the one hand, that involves a great risk of making the cat overweight; and on the other, the cat will come to do what you want only in exchange for treats. Use this type of reward only sparingly. There are plenty of other ways to reward your cat; for example, you can praise it, pet it generously, pay lots of attention to it, play an interesting game with it, or give it a new toy. You can even use a walk on a leash as a reward.

At first, favorite treats are the most effective way to get your cat to do something specific. But never use the treat as the only type of reward; always praise the cat or pet it at the same time. That way you can gradually replace the treats with words of praise, petting, and playing. The goal is to get the cat to come to you on command, perform a trick, or stop undesirable behavior.

Appropriate treats: You can get tasty vitamin and mineral tablets from pet stores and veterinarians. But even scraps of the usual dry food are gladly accepted. In addition, pieces of cheese, meat, fish, egg, or dried fish are coveted treats.

In this "Cat Track" the ball rolls very fast, but it can't come out.

A PRACTICAL LIVING SPACE FOR YOUR CAT

Cats feel quite at home in human living quarters. But in order for them to be able to play and keep appropriately busy without risk of accident or unpleasantness for humans, there are a few ground rules to observe.

Making the House Safe for Play

Tip-out windows: Tip-out windows surely constitute one of the greatest dangers to cats. A cat thinks it can get outdoors through the window; it jumps, slips, and gets caught with its neck or leg jammed ever tighter as it struggles to get free. Many cats have met a wretched death by strangulation in that way. Specialty shops sell safety devices that are easy to install on tip-out windows.

Open windows and balconies: Fresh air and sunshine are vitally important to cats. Big-city cats especially love to watch the outside world from a window or balcony. Open windows and balconies in upper-level apartments must be made absolutely safe with a cat net or wire; these are available in pet shops.

All types of "caves": Cats are all too eager to crawl into cupboards and drawers that are left open just a crack. Washing machines, dryers, dishwashers, ovens, refrigerators, and even microwaves are interesting hiding places that beckon to cats. Make absolutely sure that your cat is not inside before you close a door or turn on any type of appliance.

Water: Cats can drown in a bathtub or a large floor vase. It's a good idea to keep doors closed or keep an eye on the cat.

Hot burners: Keep hot burners covered. Cats are quick to jump onto work surfaces in the kitchen in search of edibles.

Be Considerate

Don't play your stereo at full blast in a home where cats live. That's torture for the sensitive ears of a cat. You should also cut back on perfumes and other scents and strong-smelling chemicals if the cat can't get away from them. Also, cigarette smoke is bad for your cat's health.

Electric wires: Don't leave electric wires hanging freely; many cats are tempted to bite them playfully.

Household poisons: Medicines, cleansers, laundry soaps, solvents, varnishes, dyes, and other household poisons should always be kept locked up.

Small objects that can be swallowed: Don't leave needles, thread, or pearls lying around. The cat could swallow them.

Balls of yarn or twine: Don't let your cat play with yarn or twine without supervision. The cat could strangle itself.

Poisonous plants: Be sure you don't have any poisonous plants such as dieffenbachia in the house. Pampas grass, on the other hand, is a good choice. Cats play with it enthusiastically. You also should always have cat grass available for your cat; it's available at pet shops.

Note: It's dangerous for a cat to swallow tinsel from a Christmas tree. It's best not to use it; the same applies to real candles. The cat could jump into the tree and cause a fire.

Advisory: Keep valuable objects behind glass for safety's sake. It's better to lay books flat than stand them up on places where the cat commonly jumps up onto bookcases and shelves.

Setting Up a Playground

Scratching and climbing posts: One thing you really should set up to protect your furnishings and please your cat is a multilevel scratching and climbing tree that can be purchased in many shapes at pet shops (see illustration). They come equipped with toys such as a ball or a thick rope. Observation platforms invite climbing, lingering, and watching. Cats enjoy retreating to the elevated cubbyhole for a snooze. You can also securely set up a real wood climbing tree on your cat-proof balcony.

A "cat path": A cat path can lead from an easy chair, along the walls, and over a bookshelf and the scratching post to an expanded windowsill; the artful climber can walk the route on its daily patrols (see illustration). A sheltered spot in a bookcase that offers a good view of the room may be a preferred vantage point and rest area. A secured balcony provides variety in the life of an indoor cat.

A cat feels comfortable in this apartment. Scratching and climbing posts are made more interesting with the addition of perches, cubbyholes, and toys.

Not All Cats Play the Same Way

Cats are individualists. None is just like the next one. Their preferences, their ways of playing, and their intelligence are likewise different. Something that totally captivates one cat may leave another one entirely cold. So try out several toys and discover new ways of playing with your cat that suit its nature.

Differences Among Breeds

If you get a house cat that's two to three months old, it's hard to predict whether it will turn into a temperamental bundle of energy or a more sedate representative of its kind. But with purebred cats, there are more than just major external differences. Many breeds also exhibit particular characteristics, and they have a significant effect on how the cats play.

Persians: In general these are quite reserved, deliberate, and friendly cats. Their need for exercise and their hunting instinct aren't particularly strong, and they adapt easily to indoor life. Sometimes it's not so easy to get them to play. Sometimes it seems that they prefer not to condescend to playing silly games. Wild chases across tables and cupboards are not for them. Just the same, Persians need adequate exercise to stay healthy. We need to devote a lot of time to caring for them.

Carthusians (British Shorthairs): These are likewise among the most sedate and composed cat breeds. They are also undemanding and prefer a certain amount of independence. They like to prowl around outdoors and are strong, robust hunters; at the same time, they love children and are affectionate. Carthusians that are kept indoors need lots of stimulation to play. It's best for them to live with a family.

Exotic Shorthairs: These cats are mild, pleasant, and calm—a type of Persian with short fur.

European Shorthairs: In temperament and appearance, they approximate our house cats. They play in different ways that are influenced by the surroundings in which they live.

Colorpoint and Holy Birmans: These are well suited as house cats. Both breeds are very people oriented, love children, and dislike being alone; they are well balanced and gentle, but not boring, for they like to play, even with other animals.

Siamese: These are demanding bundles of energy that require plenty of attention from their humans; their play is wild and impassioned. But they don't want merely to play, but rather to have a good time with their people, preferably all day long. Devoted as no other cats are, they are also easy to get used to walking on a leash. They can become interested

A newspaper house is a neat hiding place for little cats.

in practically all types of games, provided that their people are present. They need plenty of cuddling.

Oriental Shorthair and Brown Havana: These two are similarly temperamental and fond of playing, and are closely related to Siamese. They too require lots of attention and give limitless affection.

Balinese and Javanese: These medium-longhaired breeds, which are descended from the Siamese or Oriental Shorthairs, are equally temperamental, fond of playing, and especially devoted. They are imaginative and intelligent, and they need lots of exercise. If you're away at work a lot, they need a playmate and lots of places to climb.

Cats like toys with feathers. But these types of "birds" don't last very long.

Burmese: These are likewise very people oriented and therefore don't like to be left alone. They play with enthusiasm, if not abandon, and are gentle and persistent. They don't need to run free if you provide them with enough opportunities to play and keep them busy.

Russian Blue: A very reserved, mild mannered, friendly, and devoted cat, similar to the Korat. Both breeds like unbridled play, but are less suited to a turbulent household.

Test: How Does My Cat Like to Play?

Action	Cat's Behavior	Score
Place a large paper bag onto the floor. Then step to one side and don't pay any attention to the cat and the bag.	a) The cat sniffs the bag curiously, climbs in, pushes it across the floor, and plays with it. b) It sniffs the bag curiously, taps it with a paw, and looks hesitant. c) It walks by the paper bag and pays no attention to it.	a) 5 Points b) 2 Points c) 0 Points
Crumple up a piece of rustling paper when your cat is nearby, and drop it onto the floor.	a) The cat immediately becomes attentive when you rustle the paper and comes to the sound. It meows to get you to give it the "prey," promptly jumps for it, and plays with it on its own for several minutes. b) The cat goes over to it, swats the ball with its paw, plays with it for a moment, and then waits for you to throw it again. c) The cat looks at the ball, but has other interests.	a) 5 Points b) 3 Points c) 0 Points
Pull a toy mouse on a string and over an obstacle such as a table without letting the cat catch it.	a) The cat notices the toy mouse right away, runs after it, and follows it over the obstacle. b) The cat is interested in the "prey" and wants to catch it, but doesn't go over the obstacle. c) The cat is interested in it, runs after it, but gives up the chase when it sees that it's not so easy to catch.	a) 5 Points b) 2 Points c) 1 Point
Take an interesting toy and play with your cat. Then take it away and place it in a high place where the cat can see it.	a) The cat jumps onto the toy, brings it down, and plays with it. b) It watches you and waits for you to throw the toy for it again. c) The cat loses interest in it.	a) 5 Points b) 2 Points c) 0 Points

Test Key

15 to 20 points: Your cat likes to play a lot. It's very alert and quick to learn. If it is kept indoors, it needs plenty to keep it busy. You will have lots of fun with it.

6 to 14 points: Your cat likes to play, but is a bit reserved and cautious. It forms a very close bond with you.

1 to 5 points: Your cat is reserved by nature and isn't very fond of playing. Or else it is allowed to run free and gets plenty of exercise outdoors.

Different Feline Personalities

The various breeds are very different from one another, and they define the spectrum of characteristics of house cats. There are mild mannered, reserved, high-spirited, wild, devoted, independent, feisty, sedate, temperamental, shy, curious, fresh, and timid cats. Many have the temperament of a Siamese, whereas others embody the stoic calm of a Persian. We have no choice but to adapt the play to the cat's personality. But we can motivate fairly sluggish cats to play, provide some balance for feisty ones, and take the edge off combative ones.

Somalis: These cats are mild mannered, but they can play for a long time and are temperamental; they need lots of room to play, and prefer a large apartment with a balcony or a yard.

Abyssinians: They want lots of attention, like to play and cuddle, and are intelligent and quick to learn. They are accomplished and passionate hunters and prefer a house with a yard.

Maine Coons and Norwegian Forest Cats: It's best to keep both breeds as free-ranging cats, since they really like their freedom. In addition, they have lots of initiative and are active and clever; they like to play and have a broad repertory of tricks to keep their humans busy.

Turkish Vans: They like wild games. At the same time, these cats are devoted and don't want to be left alone. They aren't comfortable in a small apartment and should be allowed to run free.

Cats really don't hate water. They like to play with the drips from a faucet and many are very fond of drinking from it.

Many Cats Don't Like to Play

If cats show no interest in any kind of play, that's usually a sign of illness or extreme over-weight. Cats are born with an instinct for play, and they usually keep it for life.

But there are some cats, male cats in particular, that are completely healthy, and that as mature adults simply can't be motivated to play. They look at you uncomprehendingly, as if you had nothing to offer but silly child's play. They haughtily stride around their territory, set every antagonist to flight with their mere gaze, and only occasionally condescend to letting their humans give them a few strokes.

A toy hanging on a string is a real provocation to many cats.

Note: Many indoor and neutered cats tend to move less and less and greatly overeat as the years go by. They fatter they become, the less they feel like playing. Eventually they can hardly run anymore. In these cases, you need to take the initiative to motivate the cat to be more active and stay healthy. If your cat shows no interest in playing, take it for a walk, or encourage it to play with another cat, or even a dog.

Playing with Problem Cats

People and cats can't always live together without complications. Problems can arise if the cat is aggressive, jealous, shy, or timid. In many cases, great patience, firmness, and lots of attention to the cat will help. Aggressiveness, for example, is often the result of pent-up energy that's looking for an outlet. The excess energy can best be burned off in very active play sessions. But a cat can also act aggressively if it's feeling anxiety. And once it's gotten rid of its anxiety it becomes a gentle, cuddly kitten.

Helping Shy Cats Adjust

Shy cats have either had bad experiences with humans, or had no contact with people when they were young. Never try to catch shy cats forcefully, but follow this procedure:

Step 1: The cat has taken refuge under a bed or a cupboard. Leave it there and don't pay any attention to it. Place food, water, and a litter box near the hiding place. Leave it alone for several hours. Come back later and keep busy doing something without paying any attention to the cat. If possible, sleep in the same room. That is very calming to cats.

Step 2: The next morning put out fresh water and food and clean the litter box while speaking comfortingly to the cat. If the cat peeks out of its hiding place, don't try to grab it. Leave it alone awhile longer. Come back later with a toy that you slowly drag behind you on a string. After awhile tie the string and the toy to the arm of a chair so that it dangles just above the

floor in the cat's field of view. If the cat shows interest in the toy, get comfortable and remain seated.

Step 3: Try to lure the fraidy-cat out of its hiding place by using a thin branch with a flexible tip or a riding crop; slowly move the toy back and forth and make it disappear around a corner.

Step 4: Eventually the cat will carefully approach you. At first touch it very softly if it seeks out physical contact with you. This can take days or weeks.

Step 5: Offer the cat treats from your hand. Keep luring the cat and play with it without frightening it.

Step 6: Now you can allow the cat to slowly explore its new home.

Note: You can leave a radio on so that the cat gets used to hearing human voices. In extreme cases, you can use another young cat to show the timid one that it needn't be afraid of people.

Baskets of all kinds are favorite hiding places for cats.

You can use play to break your cat of undesirable behavior. But you have to be consistent; forbidden behavior must not be allowed during play.

Address It by Name

Always use the cat's name when you speak to it, and always use a pleasant tone of voice when you invite it to play, cuddle, or eat. When the cat comes on command, praise it generously. Never use its name to scold the cat; that way it won't associate anything negative with its name.

Help It Get Used to Other House Pets

The easiest way to eliminate mutual anxiety, aggression, and jealousy is to let the cat play with other animals— whether other cats, dogs, or

Helping Kittens Adjust

At first a kitten will probably seek refuge in its new surroundings under a sofa or a cupboard. Give it time to observe its new home from this hiding place. Food, water, and a litter box should be placed nearby. After a few hours you can try to lure the little one out with a toy such as a piece of yarn or a toy on a string. Pay lots of attention to it at first, and don't leave it alone at night. It misses its mother and siblings. That's how you can quickly bond with your new kitten.

A young cat can get used to a rabbit.

A toy can be used to get the cat used to the scratching tree.

rabbits. Dogs and cats are equally interested in rolling balls and other moving toys. When they try to catch the "prey," they naturally come close together.

It's harder to get a cat used to a rabbit or a guinea pig, which naturally runs away when the kitten comes close. Here you'll need lots of patience. Take the rabbit onto your lap and let the kitten get acquainted carefully. Offer them both their favorite treats at the same time (see page 23).

Toys for Cat Claws

Many cats like to use the best upholstered furniture or a good rug for sharpening their claws. Forbidding does no good unless the cat has an alternative. Give it a really nice tree, board, post, or rug for scratching. If the scratching piece is placed in a strategically favorable spot that the cat always passes on its way through the house, it probably will be accepted. Catnip spray increases its power of attraction.

If the cat fails to notice the provisions for scratching in spite of everything, a little trick will help: Slowly pull a favorite toy on a string up the scratching tree or board, and use it to motivate the cat to catch the "prey" and sink its claws into the scratching piece (see illustration above). Play only on the desired scratching piece for a while. If the cat still attacks your furniture, be firm: Say "No!" loudly and carry the cat to the right place. If necessary, you can surprise the cat with a stream of water from a spray bottle or water pistol.

Keeping a Cat from Climbing the Curtains

Curtains invite cats to climb. You may even have to temporarily tie the curtains up or remove them. Try this alternative: Hang up a burlap bag or a piece of fabric so that it hangs down to the floor. When your cat jumps up onto the curtains, take it away and place it onto the bag. Try to get it to jump onto the material and climb up there instead.

Curtains made of coarse material tempt cats to climb.

FUN CAT GAMES

It's not hard to come up with stimulating games for cats. If you watch your cat carefully, you'll surely be able to invent some good ideas for games. A good variety of toys will also help indoor cats avoid becoming bored.

Appropriate Toys

With playful cats, oftentimes all they need for a wild romp is their tail, a tree leaf, or a dangling piece of string. Everything that moves immediately attracts their attention. But of course there are plenty of other interesting toys and exciting games that cats really love.

What Cats Find Interesting

Anything that approximates prey and arouses the hunting instinct is appropriate. That means it should be movable. It should twitch, wiggle, jump, roll, or fly. Cats especially like things that crinkle, rustle, or peep. It could be a mouse! If the toy is also soft, the cat can sink its teeth and claws into it.

Professional mousers like to carry their prey off. So the toy should also be portable, not too heavy or large, and easy to pick up with the teeth.

A toy that moves and has real fur is especially attractive.

Cats love caves. On the one hand they like to hide inside them, and on the other they like to look for prey animals that use the caves as hiding places. Make-believe prey that disappear into a cave and can be brought out are very effective in heightening the hunting instinct.

But don't be surprised if after a time your cat suddenly loses interest, ignores the prey, and walks away. It has nothing to do with the toy, but is merely part of the cat's natural behavior. The desire to hunt subsides if the cat's prospects for success aren't very good. From time to time you need to let your little carnivore catch the pretended prey and toss it into the air.

Commercially Made Toys

Specialty shops offer a broad range of very appealing cat toys that are well matched to the cat's requirements.

✔ There are plush and fur mice in all types and sizes, with short or long hair, in different colors, that wind up, make noise, have little bells or squeakers, and bushy tails or feathers. Some are inside wire balls, and others are treated with catnip. This scent, which is

TIP

Getting the Cat Used to a Leash

If you can't let your cat run free because, for example, you live in an area that has lots of traffic, you still have the possibility of walking it in the fresh air and giving it the exercise it needs by using a leash (see the how-to fitness section on page 58).

Get your cat used to a harness and leash as soon as possible; both of these are available in pet shops. That way it will be more ready to accept this unaccustomed restraint. At first, keep the harness on the cat only for a few minutes and simultaneously link it with pleasant things such as treats, play, and cuddling. Then increase the use a little every day.

After about a week you can attach the leash and encourage the cat to walk forward, preferably with the help of snacks. Increase the practice time daily, always in conjunction with pleasant experiences and praise.

Then walk a few steps out the door with the cat, and give it plenty of time to take everything in. It's normal for it to seek shelter at first and want to go back inside. It should not be frightened the first time out, and it should not have any negative experiences on the leash. Avoid meeting any strange dogs, and stay away from noisy traffic. Gradually you will be able to increase the duration of these outings.

obtained from a plant, can make toys or specific places in the house especially attractive to cats. They love little bundles filled with catnip, for example. Many cats actually become intoxicated when they smell catnip. Valerian causes a similar reaction.

✔ Cats also like the many types of dangling toys that are available. They consist of a wand with a long, elastic string connected to a furry mouse. You can use these devices to make a cat pounce in the most amusing ways. Many cats like similar toys with feathers attached to them.

✔ For cats that are often left alone, there are toy mice on long rubber bands that can be clipped to door frames. All types of hanging balls and bundles of feathers serve the same purpose; these can even be attached to the cat's scratching tree.

✔ Most cats prefer soft balls into which they can sink their claws. They also like balls that are weighted unevenly, since they wobble and roll in unpredictable ways. In addition, there are balls with holes in them into which treats can be inserted. The cat will be kept busy for a long time trying to get the treats out.

✔ Burlap balls, mice, and every imaginable type of item, including scratching boards, posts, mats, and trees in all sizes invite cats to come and scratch.

There Are Cat Toys in Every House

Look around your home a little and you'll surely find a number of things that are good cat toys.

✔ A piece of crinkly or rustling paper, or thin aluminum foil rolled up into a little ball is attractive to almost all cats.

✔ Old favorites include a cork that flies around on the end of a string, or that's pulled back around a corner. Instead of a cork you can use an empty spool or a shred of fabric.

✔ Bottle caps are great fun to kick across a smooth floor with a clatter.

✔ Many cats like to chase a pingpong ball through the entire house.

✔ Of course the old ball of yarn has lost none of its attractiveness. Cats like to lie on their side and attack it wildly with their claws and teeth, just as they do with tightly rolled-up stockings. A handkerchief that's been tied in several knots fills the same purpose.

✔ Cords, string, cardboard tubes, film containers, buttons, shuttlecocks, and even dried twisted noodles and nuts can be turned into fun toys.

✔ A folded newspaper can form a roof and a great hiding place, and many cats will carry it on their back through the whole house.

✔ A little ball placed inside an empty box stimulates cats to try to get it out.

✔ An old shoe is just as interesting. It's equally difficult to get a ball out of it.

✔ Lots of cats are fascinated by cords, string, ropes, or thin belts that dangle from drawers or doorknobs. Things really get interesting when the cord becomes frayed.

✔ Many cats can't resist a running faucet and attempt to grab the stream of water.

A box with holes in it makes a very interesting playground, and not just for little kittens.

Refining Your Cat's Playground

There are no limits to your imagination as you consider possible activities for your cat. You can combine several playthings in a single game.

✔ Cats really like all types of caves and holes they can climb through. You can easily make this type of hiding place from cardboard boxes of all sizes. If you cut several different-size holes, your four-legged friend can climb in or use a paw to reach through the holes. Hide a toy inside, such as a play mouse with a bell. If there's another cat to play the game with, it will turn into a rowdy game of wrestling and catch.

I wonder if I can get such neat sounds out of this thing . . .

✔ Many cats are fond of cramming themselves into very small boxes and simply looking out. You can dangle a cat toy in front of the box and move it back and forth to lure the cat into the next game.

✔ A paper bag placed onto a smooth floor becomes even more irresistible if there is a small hole in its bottom, just large enough for the cat to stick its nose through. Wait until the house tiger scoots in, and then rustle the bag with something like a long feather. The cat will push the bag across the floor as it tries to get out the other side and seize the feather. If it really blows off a lot of steam, it may end up tearing the bag to shreds.

✔ Cats also like to play with spiders made from pipe cleaners. Take four pipe cleaners, cross them over one another, and twist them together. Wrap a fifth pipe cleaner around the middle over and under each leg and twist the ends together to make the head. Bend over the ends of the legs so they don't hurt the cat. Finally, touch up the shape of your creation. You can hang this type of spider on the scratching tree or simply place it inside a tunnel. Cats also like to carry these spiders into a hiding place.

✔ Take a large stuffed toy mouse or a wool sock filled with newspaper and use a rope and a hook to hang it in the corner of the room or from a sturdy scratching tree in such a way that it hangs some twenty to thirty inches above the floor. The cat will be so excited that it will jump up to get it, swing on it, and simultaneously sharpen its claws. The toy will be even more attractive if you attach a bell to it.

Note: You can increase the appeal of these types of toys if you spray them with catnip spray from a pet shop (see page 45).

Keeping Play Safe

Cats rarely pick up small objects, so the danger that they will swallow something is smaller than with dogs. Just the same, you should observe the following points in the interest of safety:

✔ Toys should not be capable of dissolving or consist of parts that could be swallowed.

✔ With plush mice and other stuffed toys, it's usually OK if the cat pulls them apart; they mostly contain natural materials.

✔ It could be dangerous for a cat to swallow a small ball. That's why balls for cats to play with should be more than an inch (3 cm) in diameter. Use smaller balls only under close supervision.

✔ Anything that has sharp edges or points, or that has been chemically treated, is unsuited for use as a cat toy. Such things could injure or poison your cat.

✔ You also need to be careful with the old standby of a ball of yarn. If the strands get wrapped around the cat's throat, the cat could be strangled. Let your cat play with balls of yarn and string only under supervision.

✔ Also, plastic bags that your cat might not be able to get out of and in which it could suffocate should be used as toys only in your presence.

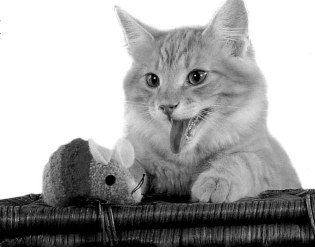

Will you play with me? I sure would like to bat this mouse around a little.

PRACTICAL ADVICE: CHILDREN AND CATS

In general, children and cats understand each other just fine. Young kittens especially find children to be enthusiastic and tireless playmates. Often times they both know intuitively what they can expect from one other.

Cats and Babies

Don't leave cats and babies together unattended. The baby could squeeze the cat or unintentionally hurt it by trying to pet it. The cat could scratch or bite as it tries to defend itself. Cats like warm baby beds. It could be dangerous for a cat to lie on a baby's chest or face. Always keep the cat's litter box and food out of reach.

This is the best way to carry a cat. It sits on your arm and its legs don't have to dangle.

What Children Have to Watch Out for in Playing with Cats

Young kittens usually take it in stride if someone plays a little roughly with them. Just the same, children should take to heart a few things in their dealings with cats:

✔ Cats need daily attention and care. You can't simply stick them into a corner like a stuffed animal.

✔ When you carry a cat, always support its body (see illustration at left); don't grab it with one hand under the belly.

✔ A little kitten can't yet defend itself. If it cries out, better leave it in peace right away.

✔ When a young cat doesn't want to be bothered, it will show that with its claws and teeth, but without really hurting you. As you play with it, you will quickly learn what it likes and doesn't like.

✔ If a grown cat feels like it's being mistreated, it can deal out some very painful blows with its paws.

✔ Cats want to sleep or rest for many hours even during

Children and cats continually invent new games. Pulling the "prey" around a corner makes the hunt a lot more exciting.

the day. Don't disturb them, or they may act surly.

✔ If your cat brings home a mouse, you shouldn't scold it. It's proud of its catch and is bringing it to you as a token of its esteem.

✔ Loud music is very painful for cats to endure.

✔ Cats are living creatures that can feel pain. They must never be pulled by the tail, and they don't like it when they are stroked against the direction of their fur. In addition, many cats have an aversion to water and don't like being bathed. Their whiskers are very important for them (see page 11) and must not be cut off.

What Adults Need to Be Aware Of

✔ Children are capable of caring for a cat by themselves starting at the age of ten or twelve. It's a way for them to learn responsibility, a sense of duty, and consideration. It's still a good idea to check up on them.

Cats don't like to be disturbed when they're eating. Children have to learn to be patient.

✔ A cat can be a good play-mate even for smaller children. Just watch how the cat reacts if the child is rough with the cat. Don't leave the two together without supervision.

✔ If there's already a grown cat in the house when a baby arrives, the cat may become jealous. Pay lots of attention to it in that case.

✔ There's no reason a healthy, regularly wormed cat free of fleas and with its shots should not sleep with an older child—provided that the child is not allergic to the cat.

Games for Cats and Children

Children usually find it quite easy to invent ways to play with cats, especially if the cat is young and responds to encouragement to play. For example, children like to push cats in doll carriages, and most cats seem to like it as well. Games of catch and hide-and-seek are part of the daily routine, as is every imaginable type of ball game. Balancing on boards and beams is among the favorite activities of cats and children. They can compete to see who can stay on longer.

Cats are only too eager to help with homework. If they become a nuisance, you have to shut them out.

What Kinds of Games Are There?

You can come up with many types of stalking, catching, and fitness games for your cat with the help of some interesting toys. In addition, you can give it tasks that require cleverness, concentration, and the ability to find things; you can practice balancing acts and work on little tricks that are lots of fun.

Walking your cat on a leash is an experience that broadens the horizons of indoor cats and helps them have fun outdoors.

Games of Stalk and Catch

Whether it involves a ball of paper, a cork, or a squeaking, catnip-filled, wiggling toy mouse, every game becomes much more attractive to a cat when you play, too. Pull a toy over the floor with short, jerky motions where the cat can see it. Stop a moment. Give your cat time to get into its stalking mode and creep up to it. Increase the excitement by moving the "prey" just a little at first, and then very fast when the cat attacks. Things get even more interesting when the prey wiggles in some harder-to-reach places rather than out in the open; chair and table legs,

corners of cupboards, doors, flowerpots, cardboard boxes, and all types of cavelike structures are perfect choices. Cats love to attack just as the quarry is about to disappear behind the obstacle or around the corner. The prey can be faster than the cat once, twice, or even three times, and get away. But then you have to allow for a little hunting success, or the cat will lose interest. The threshold lies in a different place for every cat. Older, experienced cats are quicker to give up if their efforts are to no avail; with younger cats, the fun and exercise often are more important. The cat will sink its claws into the prey, bite it, perhaps toss it up, shove it around, or try to carry it off. Then make the toy get away again, and the hunt starts all over. In increasingly exciting variations of this game, the prey doesn't stay on the floor, but rather climbs up the scratching tree, across chairs, tables, stairs, and other obstacles, and disappears under blankets, in bags, baskets, and in tunnels and pipes that you can get in all different sizes from pet shops (see the how-to section on fitness, page 58).

Many dogs like little kittens and are patient playmates.

More Games of Catch

Moving twigs: Twigs that have a long, thin, flexible tip, or a riding crop's thin end waved before the cat's eyes in a wiggling, zigzag motion before it "runs away" will almost always immediately trigger the hunting fever, no matter how reserved the cat.

Invisible prey: The little predators can't resist when the prey moves under a blanket, a cloth, or a rug. This could be a toy, a finger, or your big toe under the bed clothes. The cat lurks in its stalking stance, stares at the invisible prey, and suddenly pounces onto it.

Light games: Make the point of a laser pointer dance through a darkened room so that the cat will try to catch it. Since the cat can't

Cats and children quickly become inseparable friends.

succeed in catching the light, it's a good idea to use it only for a while and then change to a different type of prey that the cat can catch, such as a ball, a stuffed toy on a string, or a toy mouse. The cat can sink its claws into a stuffed toy as much as it wants.

Note: Be careful with laser pointers; the cat should never look directly into the beam.

container can also help prevent boredom in cats: Cut several holes in two empty, clean yogurt containers. The holes should be just big enough so that the cat can get no more than one piece of dry food out at a time. Fill one container with dry food, and glue or tape the two containers together. This requires even more cleverness on the part of the cat if the containers don't roll across the floor, but rather are hung a little over head height.

Finding treats: You can test the cat's well-developed sense of smell with another fun game. Take three boxes of different size, color, and shape that can easily be opened or that are covered only loosely. While the cat is watching, put a treat in one of the boxes. Move the boxes around several times. Now the cat has to find the right box and fish the treat out.

Searching and Thinking Games

You can even keep your cat occupied and amused if you don't simply put its food down in front of it, but make it search for it. For example, place dry food in various places around the house that are not so easy to get to so that the cat has to use its cleverness and work to get individual pieces. If you show the cat that you're hiding something, it will surely catch on to the game right away.

Fishing for dry food: Pet shops sell balls that have treats hidden inside holes; when the cat plays with the ball, the treats fall out. This food

Games for Several Cats

Once a cat has captured a valuable prey, it doesn't like to share it with another cat. It may even growl angrily if a competitor or a person comes close to take away the mouse or the pretend prey. If you want several cats to take part in a game of catch, you need more prey objects.

It's a different case with a lively ball such as a pingpong ball, though. Two or more cats will boot it around the house in a rollicking game. This game is especially fun in a fairly small, closed, empty room with a smooth floor, such as a hallway. A kitchen can also be a good arena for a cat contest. Cats also like to play in pipes and tunnels with other cats (see illustration on page 58), or in a carton with holes in it that they can use to try to catch some prey or another cat (see page 47).

Games for Kittens

Kittens love to play. They curiously approach everything that's new. Sometimes they're a little awkward and look really clumsy.

Practically all games for adult cats are equally fine for little ones. They simply can't jump as well. And their endurance and concentration are not as good as that of grown-up cats.

But in exchange, they're quicker to pitch in enthusiastically. All that's needed is a rustling leaf or wrapping paper, and the little ones attack it with gusto. They love to disappear in tight hiding places such as old shoes, boots, or wastebaskets. Toss the kitten a toy or a little ball of paper, and it will pounce on it like a wild animal.

Note: Often an exhausted little kitten will suddenly fall asleep in place. Let it take its rest and leave it alone right where it is. But if there's a danger of it being injured in that spot

(e.g., if someone might step on it), of course you should move it to some other place.

Games for Cats and Dogs and Other House Pets

Cats, dogs, and other house pets such as rabbits and quinea pigs play in different ways. That's why it's no simple matter to find something that's fun for all. But all of them enjoy games of pursuit and stalking.

Typical cat toys such as toy mice, toys on a string, and stuffed animals are best kept away from puppies, for they ruin them right away. Hard balls and pull ropes work fine for both cats and dogs. If the dog is not too rambunctious when it plays, both may even play with a toy at the same time.

Cats can balance and do gymnastics to their heart's content on a thick, tight rope.

Teaching Little Tricks

You can develop everything that cats like to do into little tricks. Just don't try to force the cat to do something against its will.

Balancing

Cats are real tightrope artists. Place a fairly long board at least four inches (10 cm) wide across two chairs. For safety's sake you should secure the board to the chairs. It mustn't wobble, tip, or slip off; otherwise the cat will become so frightened it will never again set foot on it.

Encourage your four-legged friend to walk on the plank. If it doesn't want to do that of its own will, try to motivate it by getting it to follow a toy such as a stuffed mouse that you pull along the board. Once that trick has been mastered, you can increase the level of difficulty by having the cat balance across a narrower plank.

Then you can place the board higher, for example between the scratching tree and a bookshelf.

Jumping Through a Hoop

With this favorite trick, the level of difficulty can be increased in several training sessions.
✔ At first get your cat to go after its favorite toy on a string.
✔ Then take a hoop, hold it just above the floor, and pull the toy through it so that the cat follows it, preferably several times.
✔ Raise the hoop a couple of inches. Have the cat go through the hoop again and let it enjoy the success of catching the prey.
✔ Then place two chairs about thirty to forty inches apart (80 to 100 cm). Put the cat onto one chair and use its toy or a treat as you encourage it to jump onto the other chair. Let it catch the "prey."
✔ Now hold a hoop between the two chairs and repeat the jump for the treat, as long as the cat is still game. As you do this you can gradually raise the hoop and move the chairs farther apart. Prime each jump with the command "Jump!" and at the end praise and pet the cat generously.

A toy on a string keeps the cat active while the human remains comfortably seated.

✔ Have the cat jump through the hoop to get a treat placed on the floor. Then do the same trick in the reverse direction.

✔ In the next stage of training, the cat should jump from the floor and through a hoop held about sixteen to twenty inches (40 to 50 cm) high and land on the floor.

Ideally you can stick your hand with a treat through the hoop, show it to the cat, and pull it back through so that the cat follows. Of course you praise it and reward it at the end.

Maybe the cat will learn to jump through the hoop when you give the command "Jump!"

Fetching

Dogs aren't the only ones that can play fetch. Many cats do it naturally, and enthusiastically bring you everything that they catch—including mice.

Try to get your cat to bring you the captured prey toy at the command of "Fetch!" The best toys are soft ones such as stuffed mice, since the cat can easily carry them in its teeth. If you trade a treat for it, the cat will soon understand how the game works. Then throw the toy again. After a short time you can dispense with the treat, since the game is so much fun for cats.

Standing Up on Two Legs

When cats are hunting for prey, they frequently stand up on their hind legs to seize the desired object. Put this natural behavior to good use and teach your four-legged friend this little trick: Show your cat a treat. When it goes to take it, slowly hold it higher until the cat is standing on only two legs. Say the command "Stand up!," wait a couple of seconds, and then give the cat its treat as long as it's still standing up.

Dangling toys are especially enticing. Use them only under supervision, though. The cat could get caught in a loop.

It won't take long for the cat to get the connection between standing up on its hind legs at the command of "Stand up!" and getting a tasty morsel. It's likewise possible to motivate a cat to get a treat by jumping up.

Lack of exercise and stimulation can make many indoor cats prematurely ill and fat. Your cat will remain physically fit to an advanced age if you give it a chance to play actively and keep it involved in some athletic pursuits.

Freedom on a Long Leash

One good way to give an indoor cat more activity is to take it outdoors on a fresh-air journey of discovery—on a leash, of course.

If the cat has gotten used to a harness and leash (see Tip, page 46), it still won't follow you like a dog—it's no pack animal—but it will be prepared to take you along on its stalks.

Observe the following points so that the walk will be fun for both of you:

✔ The cat determines the pace, and preferably also the direction. Under no circumstances should you drag it behind you on the leash and be impatient.

✔ A cat carefully walks a few steps and looks for cover, pauses, listens, sniffs, watches, waits, and then takes a few more steps, and so forth.

✔ You have to realize that the cat will suddenly scoot up a tree if something frightens it.

✔ Choose quiet places for your walks, such as parks or the woods. Allow time for you and your cat to play. If there's no appropriate place near where you live, take your car and drive to one.

Note: I recommend a self-retracting leash (available in pet shops) about ten feet long. A harness is better than a collar, because the cat can't slip it off.

Advice on Slimming Down Your Cat

If your cat is too fat, you should get it to play running and catching games and to go on walks; you should also cut down on its food. Give it light food (from pet shops) or have your veterinarian recommend a special diet. Hide the food in several places around the house so that the cat has to work to get it.

Playing in a Tunnel

A tunnel that's open at both ends and covered with carpeting, sisal, or artificial fur, is a favorite playground for cats. (These tunnels are available in pet shops.) Place a little ball or a toy mouse inside, and the cat will try to fish it out. It's even more captivating if you secure a toy on an elastic band inside. Cats can also roll in and on the tunnel, lie down inside to rest, and sharpen their claws on it.

A sturdy tunnel like this one is good for two to play in.

Bathtub Squash

Throw a small ball, preferably rubber, into an empty bathtub (see illustration at right). This will quickly turn into a rambunctious game. The ball bounces and rolls in all directions but can't bounce out. An equally suited squash court for this wild game is a small, closed, empty room with a smooth floor.

Obstacle Course

In your house or your yard build an obstacle course where the cat can run, crawl, balance, climb, and jump high and far. This should require practically all of its physical capabilities.

✔ Look around for anything that will serve the purpose, such as chairs, stools, stepladders, tables, cupboards, boxes, scratching tree, boards, branches or small limbs, thick ropes, and tunnels.

✔ Place the obstacles in a pattern with as much variety as possible. The course should go through the entire house. Start out with just a few stations and then add to the tasks from time to time.

✔ Be sure that all the obstacles that the cat has to jump over or climb on are solid and won't slip; otherwise the cat will become afraid of them.

✔ Get your cat interested in this course after first "turning it on" with its favorite toy and kindling the hunting flame.

✔ For one station on the course your can construct a hurdle (see illustration

Bathtub squash develops your cat's reflexes.

below) by simply joining two burlap-covered scratching boards (from the pet shop).

Pulling the "prey" over the hurdle and through the hoop—an obstacle with this type of variety is great fun for cats.

Page numbers in bold print refer to color photos and illustrations.

Abilities　10, 11
Abnormal Behavior 26
Abyssinian　39
Acclimation　42, 43
Aging Process　13
Arching the
　Back　17, **20**

Balancing　56
Balcony: Safety 34, **35**
Balinese　37
Ball Games　29
Balls　46
–, with holes **24**, 54
Biting　21, 27
Body Language　14,
　　15, 16, 17
Boxes with
　holes　47, 48
Breeds, Characteris-
　tics of　36, 37, 39
British Shorthair　36
Brown Havana　37
Burma　37

Cardboard Boxes
　with Holes　**47**, 48
Carrying　50, **50**
Carthusian　36
Catching Games　52,
　53
Cat Talk　14, 15
Cat Trail　35, **35**
Cats
–, and babies　50
–, and birds　23

–, and children　50
–, and dogs　23, 55
–, and rabbits　23,
　　42, **42**, 43, 55
–, and rodents　23
–, nervous　41
–, old　13, 31
–, shy　41
–, young　12, 13, 18,
　　19, 31
–, Toys for　**37**, 46,
　　56
Cat Track　**33**
Catnip　43, 46, 49
Caves　34, 45, 48
Cheeks, Rubbing　17
Claws　10, 27
–, Care of　10, 11
–, Sharpening 11, 17
　　21, 27, 43, 46
Cleverness　31
Climbing Tree (see
　Scratching Tree)
Colorpoint　36
Curtains,
　　Climbing　43, **43**

Dangers　49
Defensiveness　**21**
Development
　Stages　18, 19
Domestication　9

Ears　11
Electric Cords　34
European
　Shorthair　36
Exotic Shorthair　36
Eyes　11

Facial Expression　14,
　　15, 16
Fetching　57
Fitness　58
Flanks, Petting　17
Food, Hiding　54
Free-Ranging Cats　31
Fur, Care of　11

Games
– of Catch　52, 53
–, Searching　54
–, Thinking　54

Hanging Toys　**57**
Harness　46, 58
Health　33
Hearing Ability　11
Heating Elements　34
Hiding　30
Hind Legs,
　Standing on　57
Holes　34, 45, 48
Holy Birman　36
Hoops　56, 57, **59**
House Cats　26
Household Poisons　34
House Pets,
　Other　22, 23, 42,
　　43, 55
Houseplants　35

Hunting Instinct　9,
　18, 25, 45
Hunting Reflex　18
Hurdles　59, **59**

Indoor Cats 25, 26, 28
–, Neutered　40
Intelligence　31

Javanese　37

Kittens　12, 13, 18,
　　19, 31
Korat　37

Leash　46, 58
Learning　18
Learning
　Behavior　12, 13
Leg Power　10
Living Space　35, **35**
Losing Weight　58

Maine Coon　39
Mental Games　54
Muscles　10

Name, Hearing　42
Neutered Indoor
　Cats　40
Norwegian Forest
　Cat　39

Observation
  Platform   35, **35**
Obstacle Course   59
Oriental Shorthair   37
Overweight   40

Pads   10
Perches   30, **35**
Persian   **36**
Physique   10, 11
Play   18, 19
Play Behavior
  of Various
    Breeds   36, 37, 39
Playing Instinct 9, 25
Play Preferences 38,
  39
Poisons, Household 34
Posture   16, 17
Prey   45
Privacy   30
Problem Cats   41
Pupils   11

Reaction
  Speed   59, **59**
Rest   31, 32
Rewards   33
Rubbing
  – Cheeks   17
  – Head   **14**, 17
Russian Blue   37

Safety
  –, Balcony   **35**
  –, Window   34, **35**
Scent Signals   17
Scratching   27

Scratching Tree   35,
  35, 43, **43**, **61**,
    back cover
Searching Games   54
Senses   11
Siamese   36
Siblings   19, 22
Sight   11
Single Cats   26
Sleep   32
Smell, Sense
  of   11, 18, 54
Somali   39
Speed   10
Stalking Games   52
Stalking Stance   **20**
Stuffed Mice   45, 46
Swallowing
  Objects   34

Tail   16, 17
Teeth   11
Tip-out Windows   34
Toes   10
Tongue   11
Touch, Sense of   18
Toys   45, 46, 47, 48
Training   27
Tricks   56, 57
Tunnels   58, **58**
Treats   33
Turkish Van   39

Valerian   46
Vocalizations   14, 15
Voice   14, 15

Walks   28
Water   34
Whiskers   11
Window
  Boards   35, **35**
Window
  Safety   34, **35**

Yarn, Balls of 34, 47,
  49

A scratching tree should be stable and stand at least three feet high.

Helpful Addresses

American Association of
Cat Enthusiasts (AACE)
P.O. Box 213
Pine Brook, NJ 07058
(201) 335-6717

American Cat Associa-
tion (ACA)
Dept CF
8101 Catherine Avenue
Panorama City, CA 91402
(818) 781-5656

American Cat Fanciers
Association (ACFA)
Dept. CF
P.O. Box 203
Pt. Lookout, MO 65726
(417) 334-5430

Canadian Cat Associa-
tion (CCA)
Dept. CF
83 Kennedy Rd.,
Unit 1806
Brampton, Ontario
Canada L6W3P3

You can get the
addresses of cat clubs
and associations from
the foregoing
organizations.

Questions About Keeping Cats

can be addressed to
your pet shop,
veterinarian, and
veterinary associations.
Check the yellow pages
of your telephone
directory.

Pet Registries

People who want to
protect their cats from
animal thieves and
death in experimental
laboratories can register
them with various
organizations. Consult
with your preferred
veterinarian.

Helpful Books

Behrend, Katrin. *Cats.*
Hauppauge, NY:
Barron's Educational
Series, Inc., 1999.

—. *Indoor Cats.*
Hauppauge, NY:
Barron's Educational
Series, Inc., 1999.

Behrend, K. and Monika
Wegler. *The Complete
Book of Cat Care.*
Hauppauge, NY:
Barron's Educational
Series, Inc., 1991.

Church, Christine.
*Housecat: How to Keep
Your Indoor Cat Sane
and Sound.* IDG Books
Worldwide, 1998.

Daly, Carol Himsel,
D.V.M. *Caring for Your
Sick Cat.* Hauppauge,
NY: Barron's Educational
Series, Inc., 1994.

Edney, Andrew and Deni
Brown. *101 Essential
Tips: Cat Care.* DK
Publishing, 1995.

Frye, Fredric: *First Aid
for Your Cat.*
Hauppauge, NY:
Barron's Educational
Series, Inc., 1987.

Magitti, Phil. *Guide to a
Well Behaved Cat.*
Hauppauge, NY:
Barrron's Educational
Series, Inc., 1993.

Viner, Bradley, D.V.M.
The Cat Care Manual.
Hauppauge, NY:
Barron's Educational
Series, Inc., 1993.

Wright, M. and S.
Walters, eds. *The Book
of the Cat.* NY: Summit
Books, 1980.

Helpful Magazines

Cat Fancy
P.O. Box 52864
Boulder, CO 52864

Cats
P.O. Box 420240
Palm Coast, FL
32142-0240
(904) 445-2818

Cat Fancier's Almanac
1085 Atlantic Avenue
P.O. Box 1005
Manasquan, NJ
08736-0805
(908) 528-9797

Catnip (newsletter)
Tufts University School
of Veterinary Medicine
P.O. Box 420014
Palm Coast, FL
32142-0014
(800) 829-0926

The Author

Sigrun Rittrich-
Dorenkamp is a journal-
ist and editor; she lives
and works with her
husband, veterinarian
Dr. Bernard Dorenkamp,
her five children, and
many animals in
Salzkotten in Germany.
She writes for several
newspapers and maga-
zines, makes movies,
and is the author of
several books about
animals. Since child-
hood she has had a
particularly close rela-
tionship with cats, and
she currently has four
cats living in her house.
Through years of help-
ing in her husband's
clinic she has also
acquired a broad med-
ical knowledge of cats
and has had lots of
experience in dealing
with problem cats.

The Illustrator

Johann Brandstetter is a
trained restauranteur
and painter. He turned
to illustrating plants
and animals as the
result of trips to Central
Africa and Asia with
biologists. For several
years he has done
illustrations for well-
known publishers of
nature books.

The Translator

Eric A. Bye, M.A., is a
cat owner and an
accredited freelance
translator who works in
German, French,
Spanish, and English in
his office in Vermont.

Photos

Bilder Pur/MAS/Carey: page 29; Bilder Pur/Reihnard: page 32; Bilder Pur/Steimer: page 41; Binder: page 51; Cogis/Hermeline: page 20 right middle, 37; Cogis/Lanceau: page 21 top middle; Juniors/Bohle: page 61; Juniors/Born: page 20 left middle; Juniors/Heche: page 21 top left, 21 bottom right; Juniors/Schanz: page 21 left middle, 24; Juniors/Wegler: pages 9, 13, 16, 17, 21 top right, 36, 52, 57, back cover; Juniors/Wegner: page 48; Kuhn: page 25, 33, 45, 64/inside back cover; Schanz: front cover (large photo), inside front cover, 2–3, 4–5, 6–7, 8, 12, 21 top right, 20 bottom, 28, 40, 44, 49, 56; Verein Deutscher Katzenfreunde: front cover (small photo), 53.

All inquiries should be addressed to:
Barron's Educational Series, Inc.
250 Wireless Boulevard
Hauppauge, New York 11788
http://www.barronseduc.com

International Standard Book No. 0-7641-1718-1

Library of Congress Catalog Card No. 00-105830

Printed in Hong Kong
9 8 7 6 5 4 3 2

An expert answers the ten most frequently asked questions about playing with cats.

1 Under what conditions can I keep a cat indoors all the time?

2 How long should I play with my cat?

3 What do cats like to play with?

4 Why do cats play with their prey?

5 Why doesn't my cat like its toy anymore?

6 Can cats be trained?

7 What can I do to keep my cat from scratching when I play with it and pet it?

8 Can little children play with cats?

9 Isn't it better to have two cats so that they can play with each other?

10 Do older cats still like to play??